Angles of Disorder

Zachary C. Bush

BlazeVOX [books]

Buffalo, New York

Angles of Disorder by Zachary C. Bush
Copyright © 2009

Published by BlazeVOX [books]

Printed in the United States of America

Book design by Geoffrey Gatza
Cover art by Krista Schlueter

First Edition
ISBN: 9781935402169
Library of Congress Control Number 2008943146

BlazeVOX [books]
14 Tremaine Ave
Kenmore, NY 14217

Editor@blazevox.org

*p*ublisher of weird little books

BlazeVOX [books]

blazevox.org

2   4   6   8   0   9   7   5   3   1

B   X

Acknowlegments

Some of these poems have previously been published by: *Promethean, Gold Wake Press, Miscellany, The Externalist, Dogzplot, Lamination Colony, AGUA, Word Riot, JUICE Online, Calliope Nerve, VOX Press, edifice wrecked, Pudding House Publications, Mud Luscious, R.KV.R.Y Quarterly, Instant Pussy, Scintillating Publications, Mad Swirl, PEQUIN, Willows Wept Review, decomP,* and other fine small press literary venues.

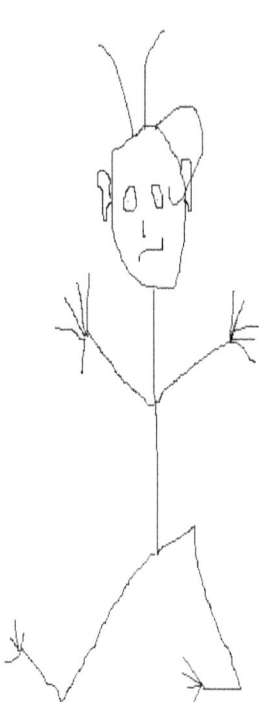

Table of Contents

This collection is for Krista, my loving parents, and the memory of Peter Christopher.

Angles of Disorder

Illumination

The Ferris wheel spins–yellow, orange, and red against the night. Her palm is sticky from ice cream dripping over the cone. The smell of hot dogs and funnel cakes thicken the air. A carnie shouts, "Double or nothing!" Her lips taste cotton candy sweet. We look up at heat lightning filling the sky.

The Ferris wheel keeps spinning–our whole world is now.

Within the Within

In the middle of the night, when That Which Reassures Us In Our Dreams had drowned in your veins, you woke up screaming. In the middle of your screaming, you looked towards the foot of the bed, where you saw two tall curtains opening. In the middle of the opened curtains, a large and unfamiliar theatrical stage was revealed to you. In the middle of the stage there stood a giant easel facing a silent audience. In the middle of the easel rested a 40x60 in. piece of cardboard canvas. In the middle of the cardboard canvas was a painting of a black-swirl sea. In the middle of the sea between claw-curled waves there bobbed a tiny red sailboat. In the middle of the tiny red sailboat sat you, so small, staring at me, staring at you.

AN INTRODUCTION TO HUNGER

For 68 days his dreams were highlighted in The Four Colors of Hunger, and so the man spent all his half-waking hours walking down and up The Avenue of Appetites – in search of **EVERYTHING** – fearful of the few short feet planted between him and the brilliant pale-blue hue of **NOTHING**.

CONCLUSION:

Urged on by his Great Nutritional Despair, the man returned to the house of his dead mother–*his once-a-breathing-genius-of-a-mother*–where he proceeded to eat 29 tall stacks of $1 notebooks; thousands of college-ruled lines, filled with her original algebraic formulas: his childhood memory…memories: symbols, figures, and numbers; numbers, numbers, numb… and number.

The Traveler

After seven months of eating nothing but walnuts and moths, the old man, having felt too confined to his living room, stepped into his bathroom and sealed the Velcro door. Once inside, loud Salsa music flooded the bathroom. The old man stood still, looking all around the empty space, trying to find where the music (which he decided that did not like in the least) was coming from. Unable to locate the music's source, he decided to close his eyes and count backwards from 49 to 42.

When the old man opened his eyes, he quickly realized that the Salsa music would probably not stop just on account of him closing and opening his eyes. The old man somehow knew that he wasn't all that powerful, so he turned his crooked back to the light and faced the shower. After allowing his tired eyes to adjust to the lesser light, he began studying the shower curtain. The old man, who still had a tendency of letting life shock him, was not at all surprised by what he saw in front of him. He softly exhaled and said, "Well, today I am a snake, but what will become of me tomorrow?"

Without takes his eyes off of the shadow, the old man reached over for the razor that rested on the sink counter. He gripped the razor-back tightly in his hand and brought it back to face the curtain. Without pausing, he began cutting a hole into the curtain. Once he had shaped and sized the hole in a way that he liked, the Salsa music suddenly stopped.

The old man dropped the razor to the ground and ran his hands through his long grease-white hair. He looked once more around the room, and over his shoulder, to make sure that no one else had entered the room. Once satisfied with his solitude, and accepting of his dire situation, the old man decided that what he was about to do would be for the best.

The old man took one last breath and slowly poked his finger into the hole. Once he felt his finger on the other side, he pushed his head and chest through, and then his legs and feet, followed finally by his toes, until his entire body had slithered through The Hole.

<u>From the center of The Circle</u>:

a realization, a lit fire, a star tax, & yesterday's transglobal conference call. Far too worn out from revising Information. This BE a Form Life – repeating the repetition. A fire = flames. Of flames – Of flames – Oh flames – These flames! I took a Polaroid picture of the flames and a T.V. appeared in the framed box – sudden Realism, sans uniform. An aquatic vocal distortion. Salt-stitched into sudden moment monument's EyeSight. Disintegrate 2 reintegrate: loose goose bumps, (time-released) slow burning villages, delusional corner-rounding rounded corners, fragmented translations of untranslatable cultural catchphrases, and distant crops that grow out of Curious George corpses. A Sing Song Lullaby, revived and digitally remastered. Mechanical clapping computer. Overweight Water Queen, sobbing Top 50 Doo-Wop Hits. Sketching the differences in U.S. Stop Signs. An American Flag waxed in yellow wax hangs still-to-still-life. The flag hangs 8 ½ feet above a village of matchstick castles, unable to melt because of the confused conversion. That, most likely, was just another Blackout contortion. See: no breeze, no sound, & nothing near to sestina humidity. Yet, something is sweating. Wax sings: drooping, dropping, releasing, & splattering onto the sand. The sand, that resembles volcanic ash, covers the ground. Aquarius has gone tonight. 'A' is as realized now. I see the all-consuming Frequency (trying like a bastard) to consume me…***constantly dreaming in circles.***

The [Related] Parts of a Family

When The Girl walked into the living room, after nearly a year away from her home, she would have never expected to have seen her father doing anything more than eating potato chips, and masturbating in front of the space heating unit. So, The Girl must have been thoroughly shocked when she saw her father dissecting an accordion on the rug. This new living room scene had already been quite enough for her, but it did not help the matter that the accordion moaned like – it moaned like someone she thought knew at one time – every time her father sliced through its insides with his scalpel. Yes, this did not help with her current anxiety in any sort of way. Surely confused and probably resentful, The Girl said to her father, "Father, why are you dirtying your gentle hands in the bowels of this whining accordion." She paused a moment to catch her breath, shook her head, and then she asked, "And *why* does *this accordion* cry like a human…I…know…when…you…Why?"

Never looking up at The Girl, but vaguely recognizing her voice as his daughter's voice, the father just shook his head. He grunted something inaudible. He then raised the scalpel to his prickly chin, scratching at it with the dull-side of the blade. He cleared his throat, and then yelled, "for The Love of Family, I dirty my hands; for The Love of Gender Studies, I dirty my hands; for The Love of All Who Protest The Re-Production of Tennis Balls, I dirty my hands; for The Love of Infinity, I dirty my hands; for The Love of Hitler, I dirty my hands; for….I…" The father looked up and was now staring at his daughter full-on, and from his lips came a near-muted phrase. The Girl took the silent movements of his lips to mean- *come closer*, and so she did just that. The father scratched his head with the scalpel, and said, "This is no ordinary Bavarian accordion, this is…this *was*…this *in fact*…is your Uncle Morton, before he…well, before we…no, he…before we changed into…what he is now… all for The Love of Undiscovered Animal Anatomy!"

The Girl stood, as if she cemented to the rug, still in shock. She stared in a dead-pan silence at her father who had since re-buried his head into the metal-belly of the instrument. She thought…*her uncle: hated, a life expired, now transformed and still moaning like the bastard that he is…was…*And with this a red-water relief rushed over The Girl's forehead. She probably instinctually knew that she needed some air and so she went into the front yard. Once between the mailbox and the garden that hugged the jaw of the house she collapsed backwards onto the grass. She started shrieking, laughing like her schizophrenic accordion of an Uncle. Her face contorted like ocean waves. She began tearing up the grass from the ground, stuffing handfuls of it down her pants, and even deeper into her panties. The Girl screamed, "For The Love of Microcosms, indeed; for The Love of Solar Eclipses, indeed; for The Love of Cats, indeed; for The Love of Underground Robotics!"

In the living room, The Girl's father could hear his daughter screaming in the front yard. He found that he was heavily torn between continuing with what he knew was the best course of action (for all that he praised) – the dissembling and dissecting of Morton – and reassembling his brother back to life. Yet, he didn't falter. He said, "For The Love of Suppressing Morton's Madness for Mathematics, I dirty my goddamn hands!"

A LESSON IN BREATHING

One morning, when the boy was nearly ten years old, his father woke him, and said, "Son, we're leaving for the mountains." And so they left.

Later that morning, as they crossed into the neighbor's yard, his father pointed to the mountain range that circled the city and said, "Out there will be our new home." The boy nodded, and they walked into the mouth of the woods behind their neighborhood. Father and son hiked a few sluggish miles before they came to a lake; frozen, at the foot of the nearest mountain. They sat down to rest. Not long after his father fell asleep, the boy tried to masturbate beside the lake, but nothing came of it, so he listened to the ducks squawking and cursed his penis.

Later that afternoon, when they were three quarters of the way up the mountain, they stopped again for water and rest. The boy's father turned to him, dried his face of sweat, and said, "Last night I gagged your mother and locked her in the attic." The man then asked his son if he cared to know why he had done it. The boy looked at him and said, "Indeed, I *would* like to know why you did such a thing." The man took a quick swig from his canteen before looking out over the city where they used to live. He said, "Because she laughed too much and for far too long at times when she shouldn't have…"

Later that night, as the boy's father tucked him into his sleeping bag and kissed him on the forehead, the boy laughed out loud at the thought of his mother's hot, muffled screams. But he tried not to laugh for too much or for too long, because he was a severe asthmatic.

From Within the Vortex

The Boy knew *it wasn't really his fault*, not as it pertained to reality, anyways.

As usual, try blaming it on The Parents—Mother...*Mother? ...Mother!*

"No one has any goddamn control over the day they're born," his Uncle would say.

But what difference does that make really...really?

Wait, I thought I saw...wait, what was that...wait, a shadow, maybe...?

The Boy always knew that life would be tougher for him than it would be for The Others.

"Well, what difference does it all make?" His Uncle would ask.

Yes, much, much shorter.

But what control did The Boy have over his eyes first opening the day The Sun died?

By the age of 5, The Trees had all withered dry, snapped, and keeled over.

Everything was black, always.

The Boy has no control over these things...nothing.

There was nothing to see, there is nothing to see, but that was fine, but that is fine.

The Boy plays guessing games with his Uncle's memories—life before his own.

His Uncle: black. His parents turned black before he could remember, like everything.

Nothing has changed anything...not for The Boy...not for the life he does not see.

Cursing the Gods of Higher Calculation

His life was never meant for exponential functions,
Nor should it have ever been part of the Universe's
Plan for him to have aged into a Schizophrenic Logarithm:

Cold   *&*   *Lost*

The Difference

He met She on the day of Sixteen Hours. That day, like many days, was one of the longest He had ever experienced. No matter how hard He thought about it, He couldn't put his foot on exactly why it seemed so tortuously long. But He knew that He was just like all The Others; He too never questioned The Clocks and never cursed The Calendars.

It was sunny that day, yet there were a few lightly scattered clouds. He wasn't sure how the weather factored into the day, but that was what it was like around the time She walked into He's vacuum repair shop.

According to the judgment of The Clocks, one-fourth of the day had since elapsed, but to the townsfolk it felt like noon. Yet on that day, as with most days, He was just like all The Others who never compared actual time with intuitive time. No one thought there was anything the wrong with the day, even if it was built with Sixteen Hours.

She was incapable of blending in with the vacuums like all The Others, and He found He-self staring straight at She; leaned against a wrong-wired vacuum. She was screaming to Everyone, Anyone, and No One; whoever might listen. She was obviously upset with the townsfolk. He sensed this as she accusingly screamed, "HASN'T ANYONE, EVERYONE, AND NO ONE NOTICED THAT OUR SIDEWALKS ARE SIDE-SLANTED 3.3 DEGREES?"

Neither Everyone, Anyone, nor No One responded to She's cries, because the vacuum repair shop was empty outside of He, and He was utterly mesmerized by She's acute awareness of real-life algebraic scenarios. He confirmed this impression by whispering it into He's knotted beard. He had never seen such a thing as She.

Not knowing what to say to She, He asked, "WOULD YOU CARE FOR A PINE-NUT MINT?" He asked. But She, realizing that He had been listening-in on her questioning – questions that She believed She had not intentionally addressed to He – scoffed and turned away from He. "I ONLY SMOKED IT ONCE," she confessed, "LOGIC, THAT IS, I WOULD…"

"LIKE TO PET MY PET CRAB?" He asked She. "HIS NAME IS RUSSELL." In response to He's attempt at conversation, She began to knock over He's vacuums one-by-one. Finally, in a glaze of sweat, She shouted, "IT'S ILLEGAL YOU KNOW…" Amazed, He said, "Nothing…." He just stood as still as He could in the shop. He knew not whether what She had said was True or False. "IT WAS BY MISTAKE," She pleaded, "I NEVER KNEW IT ACTUALLY WAS WHAT IT WAS AND NOT WHAT I POSSIBLY WANTED IT TO BE, JUST FOR ME AND NO ONE ELSE. IT JUST DOESN'T WORK THAT WAY!"

He continued to stare at She as He backstepped towards the cashier's drawer. Again, not knowing what more to say or how to react to She, He reached into the cash drawer and pulled from it Giant Calculator. He bet himself that She would have never guessed that He was quite musically inclined, but now He would show She with Giant Calculator. He stood tall as She watched He, towering over the largest calculator she had ever seen. Not knowing what to do, and not having any more vacuums to knock over, She reached into Pant's Pocket and pulled from it a long butter-knife. He watched She from the corner of He's eye as He commenced to play Giant Calculator's keys.

She held the knife horizontal to She's lips and smiled a lovely mechanical smile, like that of an exquisite corpse. And, like He has been prone to do with The Others, He mistook this smile for an intense ecstasy for He and Giant Calculator's music and so He played the calculator louder and louder. She stared at the blurry face in the butter-knife, occasionally obscuring the reflection to pick at front teeth. She never looked up from the knife. And then He, realizing that She had smoked LOGIC and had realized how empty it was, began to cry loudly. She continued to smile into the side of the butter-knife. Giant Calculator never ceased to miss a beat.

Silence in the Gutted Fields

This is really no worse than the wormhole you packed me in, I whispered, running my boney fingers through his greasy gray hair. . .

Yet, how can I ever expect him to comprehend who I am, if I never speak my thoughts? Still, I watched him cry when I dug my long yellow fingernails into his marble-white eyes, and though he screamed loud, louder than his father burning, I couldn't bring myself to stop.

I felt nothing but contemptuous hate and **Nothing** *could bring about any softening to my heart, not in me, no! not even an all knowing smile as we laid, naked, side by side, sweating in the gutted fields between a 55 foot stone cross and a red dilapidated barn, between the* **beyond** *of this highway, beyond, beyond the red, beyond the blue-*

Truth.

The rain fell and hit my face, each drop rolling down my chin and onto my chest, sliding green down my ribs.

My father is long dead... his eyes I ripped from the sockets. Now he speaks to me in ancient tongues and I float on three inches of green, green rain.

Symbol.

If you go *out there* to look and can't find him where I say he be, then don't come back here, doubting me.

The Wet Season

When the rains finally died, I blinked and realized I'd lost Time. During the lapse, other things appeared to be lost to me too: father, mother, sister, brother, wife and... I?

Where is father?
Where is mother?
Where is sister?
Where is brother?
Where is wife?
Where is Time?
Where is 'I'?

The rains, the rains-- I lost it all to the rains!

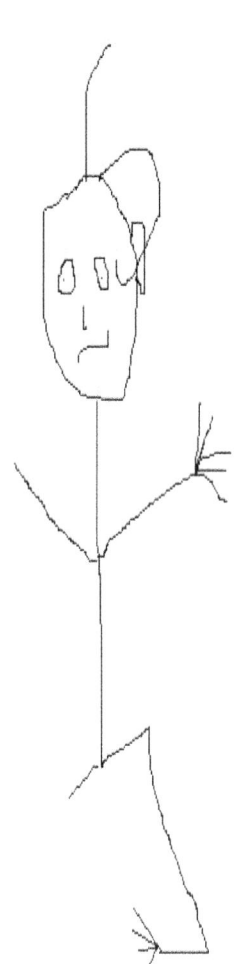

The Horse

On my seventeenth birthday, my Uncle Morton built a carousel in the middle of my bedroom. Morton, as he did with many things, mistook my obsession with numbers to be one for plastic, smiling horses. I am almost positive I never asked him to take on such a ludicrous feat, but no one can stop a man who has spent 16.95234 years in a basement, feasting on thousands of ripe tennis balls, from building a carousel for his teenage nephew.

Maps That Spin

When our first opportunity for help was lost in the yellow reflectors, we were discovered, trapped inside the colorful shadows of sound. We would have shattered green glass screens if we could have... because the television always mimicked purple thighs opening – a tomorrow's mouth.

When Mercury was found to be in its final stage of retrograde, that's when we turned towards the kitchen clocks for definite answers. But those clocks were so wise! Somehow they always discouraged impatience and vanity.

Maybe they knew my defects better than I did. Maybe

tonight we should close our eyes and slide forward. Maybe

tonight we will pack ourselves into these steel time capsules.

The Catch

I once knew a girl who, having grown so terribly resentful towards The Sun, stole her father's dwarf-moose trap, and set it on her desk calendar. The girl, typically known for her extraordinary high level of impatience, was suddenly overtaken by a most unusual wave of calmness. Eager for a catch, the girl spent the next three days staring at the open jaws of the trap.

Early in the morning, on the fourth day, the girl was startled awake by the sounds of something screaming, "6, 7, 8, 9…10:00 AM!" The girl jumped out of bed, and ran over to her desk calendar, where she found Thursday trapped and flopping between the shiny metal jaws of the trap. Thrilled at the sight of her prize catch struggling in front of her the girl decided to spend all of Friday (which would have normally been Thursday if Thursday had not been caught in her trap) smoking a cigar, and watching Thursday bleed to death.

When Thursday had finally passed, the girl drifted into a deep contemplation. After a few hours, she came out of her trance. It was then, and only then, that the girl realized she now possessed enough confidence to try to next catch The Sun. Though, the next time, she knew she would need a much larger moose trap.

MEMORIES FROM THE HOUSE OF BENDING MIRRORS

Purple legs hang limp over the side of a giant wine glass

Spiders eating spiders on the kitchen countertops

Your brother made a nice shrimp cocktail

Books somersaulting down the stairs

Shuffling naked across the blood-sticky linoleum floor of the kitchen

Father at the dinner table on the phone with Jesus in Beijing

The bedroom that reeked of spoiled grapes

Swastikas spinning on the ceiling

Indians making bets from behind holes in the walls

Running a comb through cotton candy

Grandmother kissing a cracked-frame picture of Lenny Bruce

Sister cutting cats out of satin sheets

Dead fish rotting in the bathroom sinks

Eating mothballs to test the angel theory

Dissecting flies with rusty thumbtacks

Your grandfather beating the radio in chess

A ceiling fan tutoring you in Spanish

Bathing for hours in cold split-pea soup

Encyclopedias rewriting themselves in Sanskrit

Staring out stain-glass windows waiting for The Sun to explode

Listen, listening, always [careful] listening

The Final Action of turning her Will and Life over to the care of THE COUNSEL OF ECHOES scared The Old Woman so much that she began screaming loudly; with as much intensity, and consistency as was possible with her aging lung capacity.

In the meantime, her screams had excited THE COUNSEL OF ECHOES so much that they began to reproduce and return the horrific pitches back to the earth as quickly as was possible with their great sound-reproduction team's prolific capabilities.

But what The Old Woman was letting loose, in all her agony, was nothing like any of the other billions of men, women, animals, and children's screams that THE COUNSEL OF ECHOES had ever heard. And it wasn't much longer before their great sound-reproduction team realized that even *they* could not keep pace with the intensity of The Old Woman's unusual sound production. They figured that something must be done as soon as possible...but...what?

Completely unaware of the much larger situation at-hand, and as mortified as ever by her thoughts of The Final Action, The Old Woman would not allow herself to stop screaming; not for anyone, or anything. So, she screamed, and screamed, and screamed until she was transformed into a gigantic whirlpool of sound. And at that very moment– her moment of sudden transition– The Old Woman silenced every last member of THE COUNSEL OF ECHOES...along with herself.

Our Youth

I once knew a boy who grew so desperate for disharmony that he tried to masturbate with a frozen banana. Afterwards, while in the shower, the boy felt so greatly dissatisfied with the act, that he saw no other option but to sew his osteoporetic grandmother to his father's back.

Not too long after the boy did this, he felt even worse, and grew more desperate than ever before. He began to have uncontrollable cravings for much greater disharmony, so he tried swallowing WEDNESDAY and choked to death.

When They Come Inside

You will burn white, like the _____
They will sprinkle into your open wounds.

You will bubble and boil
Up over the surface without a cry…

You have forgotten what it means to fight.

But what about The Feral Cat that is crippled?...the one that hides in the undercarriage shadow of our cart on hot summer afternoons... those days when we would melt if we crossed the threshold of our front door.

But what about the Ghost of a Man in our living room, who is constantly adjusting the radio dials (that only he can see) ... and all those conversations he has (talking with himself) about FDR and the New Deal. This man had no legs... So, can we really deny him of that fact? Do you not believe he cut them off to help us better breathe… at this exact moment?

Angles of Disorder

Aged and weary from traveling through The Hole…The Traveler sat on a yellow curb, in a parking lot outside of a diner, watching two dogs go at it; mauling the hell out of each other. And thick clumps of blood wet-stained their raised hair. But this primal brawl was of no real concern to The Traveler at the moment. He had more important things on his mind, like the little old woman, sitting on the hood of her lime-green Chevy Nova.

The Traveler was intensely annoyed with this woman, because no matter how hard he tried to think about it, he couldn't figure out why she seemed so happy; why she appeared so incredibly ecstatic. With all the violence in the world, what could produce such happiness in any human…especially happiness within this little old woman?

This truly frustrated The Traveler to no end, until he decided to ask her about it.

"Old woman," The Traveler said, "what in the Blue Heavens has got you so giddy?"

The little old woman looked straight at him. She smiled and let her eyebrows rise and fall some, before reaching into her pocket. She brought out a crumpled Carnival Finger.

The little old woman held the red-wrinkled stump up to The Sun, and shouted, "This, this right here be ma' Wishbone!"

The Traveler stared in silent awe at the stump of the Carnival Finger, watching the sunlight reflect off of it. He couldn't help but smile at the luck of this little old woman, and within seconds The Traveler became quite fond of her.

But, no sooner did The Traveler and the little old woman share in their moment of common joy, than did two vicious dogs catch wind of her prized Carnival Finger…and then five minutes elapsed…and what happened in between that time added up to equal the end of the little old woman and her luck. So, The Traveler, having nothing else better to do, left the diner parking lot in search of others.

The Retired

There was an old couple who truly loved birds. In fact, I have never met two people who loved birds as much as this old man and his wife.

On Sundays you could usually find the old man at the local store, laughing with the young girls behind the registers, and trying to strike a deal over half a pound of seed.

Every afternoon—no matter the weather—he and his wife could be seen from the road, standing under the feeder in their front yard, chatting with the birds. By night the couple would invite the birds into their home (usually 10 or 12 at a time) to perch around them at the dinner table.

One evening, after the two had spotted me on the road, I was invited to join them for supper. After much food, and much whiskey —generously poured by the old man's hand —the old wife asked me if I'd care to follow her, her husband, and the birds, into the bedroom, to put a stamp on their joyous occasion.

The Last of the Caged

The Instructor and The Boy were exhausted. For nearly six hours they had been sitting at a small table, in an otherwise empty classroom, staring at one another in complete silence. The Instructor had been quite frustrated with The Boy's silence, but after meditating on the various pros and cons of speaking up, he had convinced himself that it might be best to talk to him.

The Instructor rubbed his dry eyes before looking at The Boy. "Pick up your pencil and notepad," he sighed, "and draw, for me, however it is you see me." The Boy slowly nodded his head. He glanced at The Instructor, then at the blank notepad, and then again at the old man. He repeated this process four or five more times, before lowering his head, and commencing to draw exactly what he saw.

While The Boy drew in his notepad, The Instructor gazed out the classroom window. On a large oak branch, just on the other side of the window, he had spotted ten sparrows, lined up in a row, facing his gaze. He exhaled loudly, and stared down the line at their twenty beady eyes. Sensing the sparrows' suspicion and their growing anger, he became terribly bothered, and shook his head. He was confused. He thought to himself - *these sparrows are not at all as pleasant as they ought to be!*

After another minute had elapsed, The Instructor turned his attention away from the birds. Looking at The Boy, he realized that his drawing-time was over. The Instructor tapped his fist against the table, and to The Boy he said, "Well, what do you have for me...come on and turn it over." The Boy, never looking up at The Instructor, handed his notepad to him. He then gathered his belongs, and stood. He stared down upon the little old man on the other side of the table.

The Instructor held the notepad close to his eyes for a review. When he caught sight of what the boy had scrawled, his hands began to shake violently. He held the page closer to his eyes, but everything went to blur. He squinted, trying make-out the number 8450929143287567821312004499.34 that had been written, in repetition, from the top to the bottom of the first eleven pages. The Instructor's splotched-red face quickly turned to ash gray. He looked up at The Boy in horror, but The Boy did not seem to care; he was out of sight.

The Boy had just walked out of the classroom and down the hallway, when The Instructor began to let loose hideous screams; and he had not made it past the fourth classroom by the time he heard a great shattering of glass, the sharp cracking sounds of tree limbs snapping, and the long drawn-out echoes of the sparrows chirping...*chirping*....chirping....*chirping*....

Le Noyé

The Boy swam at dusk, while I dreamt of spreading muddy sand across the surface of The Sun. He had no time for dreams, this boy. He never feared The Sea, slipping in between the waves.

I rubbed my eyes with sandy fingertips, and he was gone.

THE EMERGENCE OF A NEW INSTITUTION

When The Woman's electric kazoo had ceased to amuse the High Court of Lorta, she was stood before The Queen.

For having no eyes, ears, nose, lips, or mouth; Her Majesty had a most extraordinary view into the human condition. This was proven to The Woman when The Queen, who had sat silent throughout the whole musical performance, handed The Woman a silver notepad. On the first piece of paper, in blackened block letters, the faceless queen wrote:

WHY ARE YOU SO JEALOUS OF THE BASHFUL FOX WHO CROCHET'S MAJESTIC HOLIDAY SOCKS?

The Explosion

Some weeks after it happened, The Woman would tell them that The Fall felt just like biting into a crisp-cool wedge of Iceberg lettuce…that is…it would have been exactly that way if her *entire* body had been a complete set of teeth and oral nerves. She would then say that she couldn't remember the specifics of The Landing – her Final Impact – but that part didn't matter much anyways. What *was* important was what came next.

The Great Explosion of Morning Dew had taken her by surprise, The Woman would say to *them*, sounding at first like machine guns being fired by a subterranean gang of lawn moles, perhaps. But, The Woman realized that she had felt no hot bullets penetrate her skin. Then she thought The Explosion sounded like the simultaneous uncorking of thousands of champagne bottles. She thought of New Years' past – her dead father, husband, and his sister – and The Woman began to weep uncontrollably.

And The Woman was still weeping when the neighbor's son found her in the front yard. She was naked, and curled-up like a broiled shrimp, shielding her eyes from the silver-sparkling blades of his father's prize-winning Bermuda grass…

Recalling BUGGERSENSE

Every day is set to the default mode, 'Tuesday Morning.' But, there has been a great wet-wire malfunction– & some innocent people have been mutilated in the process, maybe– so, regardless, Today is now 'Monday Morning.'

Last night I dreamt that the cryogenic freezing process was invented during the times of The Epics. There had been only two accepted applicants: Homer & James Joyce. The Gods of Cryogenics were, back then, no more than amateur optometrists... but they were very hopeful towards advances in 'sight' in the future. When Homer & James Joyce thaw, with a new vision, the world will be nicely wrapped!

-that was my
dream…

At 9:13, I awoke to a putrid smell. Within a period of forty-six seconds my solitude turned so thick that I couldn't breathe without violently beating my chest. I reached my hand out, to take a sip from the cat, but my cat was stretched across a gold-print shopping bag. My cat is quite busy these days…late stages of feline rigor mortis.

My head itches, my head itches so intensely, and, so, I scratch it. My hair is a fetus corpse. There are ash deposits under my fingernails. This description is precise and it is exact: my brain is burning, literally, too much talking going on in my mind. *Hear the bubble?* I can feel the static-stench of nerve-endings popping my eyes. *I realize.* Not enough time to digest all of this now... The bugs are coming out. I feel their sound patterns, vibrating, and waving across the room, like checkerboard syllables, hopscotch, and baritone chess matches.

The Vortex opens its funnel overhead, and here they come: the bugs! I watch them tip-out: rose chafers and rustic moths; root weevils and modern beau weevils; rust-red beetles and blood-red-tailed bumblebees; a north American yellow jacket and one, two, three more; redcurrant fire-flies and sucking louses; thirty-seven trilobites and some scabies mites; social wasps!

On Tuesday's I usually go to the park for relief from my mind. The park is where I always witness events that restore me to sanity. Today there is a teenage boy sitting on a west-end bench. When I reach him, he carefully picks up The Great Eight Colors and shuffles them between his fingers, and as I watch, there is a magnificent melding, churning, bleed-on-bleeding discovery—infinity, realized—THE BIRTH OF TA-PHO-RA!

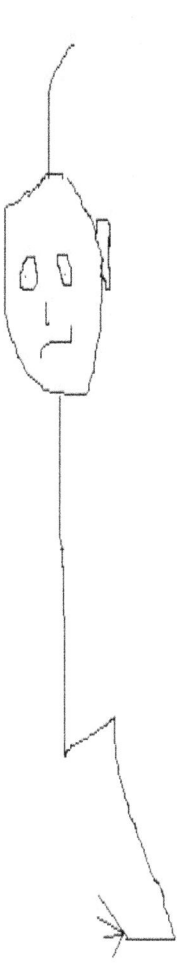

The Numerologist Who Converted [1]

And when he left the numbers, his friends left him...

He now spends all of his hours, alone, in a room filled with broken calculators and shattered grandfather clocks, happily reading the collected works of a poet, who had dedicated his entire life to The Sun, and all the great myths that further support and sustain its furious glow.

THE SUN first began by working him from the inside out, and then THE SUN continued on him from the outside in, and when THE SUN presented him with sweet opportunities of total nonsense, he began to fear that he would not make it through **The Hours of the Night**, without at least one bright-light orgasm.

While The Seasons passed one by one, **THE SUN** (having less and less time to dedicate to The Newly Converted Astronomer) proved to be the laziest of lovers; *at least in the eyes of the mortal one.*

With all this pain, the numerologist became so terribly depressed by the growing distance between himself and **THE SUN**, that, out of a total desperation, he turned his total dedication back to the numbers, but they paid him no more attention. This made him sadder than ever.

Late one night, before **THE SUN** awoke, the numerologist figured it would be best if he gouged out his eyes…with a spoon…and so he did.

DNIWER TXE UE

I.   ovarian circu-soar____$5 a tongue root(s) bind us blind

II.   annexed restitution sewing daz decay = freedom for........?

III.   thumbnail blackout welcomes rusted machines

IV.   Balzac alchemists submerging The Flag for The Flag

V.   elitist somersault in that greeeeeeeeeeeeeeeen misery

VI.   forlorn chronology and the babies? WhateverwasSafe is____

VII.   bourgeois birds expelled from my mouth severin sivran circlejerk

VIII.   garlic tumbler embrace _____entrapment squared

IX.   Quevedo invited Zufransia in   to   and Gongora's ear

X.   Emblerza / / [wilter]

This Little Red Balloon

From her living room floor, he can hear the vibrations of her memory's static-grain state; reoccurrences, like a present tense talk-show host, manically announcing that the world's rarest palate of paint was consumed by a magnificently tortured skeleton in St. Petersburg, in his final attempt at recreating *Silver Dusk*.

For now, let's understand this static to be nothing greater than whatever it means to this man to exist within red-painted Mylar; an abrupt fade-out frequency tuned to a near-lost AM radio station of an eager school of Alaskan salmon swimming upstream.

She would probably doubt he has much of a will; but, he can smell hers'. It is like a purple sheepskin glove, straddling the touch-n-spark subway tracks of his yesterday's dream.

And, in regards to his mind, all should grant him submission; the kind one would grant something that is already dead.

From Beneath His Mountaintop

Red-bearded hyenas tear into zebra loins; all Lion left over. Their flesh rips and pops, like a thousand rubber bands released at once.

Untitled Dream That Led Me to Stop Believing

Half asleep walking through paths of ash and broken glass the wind whips the tops of the waves. I hear the howling of the winter winds and feel sticky sand between my toes. These Elders, pale and thin, are crouched behind the high-reed, rolling dunes. They are watching me, watching The Girl, watching the blue-skinned children wash up with the stain-red tide.

The sea recedes back into its gut. The air reeks of rotting fish and burnt eggs: my many nightmares of you. And I am falling while standing up.

I awake, and touch the soles of my burning feet --*they are caked thick with the ash of the dead.*

Before The Grand Ascension

This is the hour when the heavens birth a full Moon to share sky with The Sun. This is The Hour when two children rise from the town's sewer caps, like lit candlesticks.

They can sense dusk from within their canals of shit. But, now they're drawn to a new scent; the decaying of stranger-s-bodies, wrapped in black polyurethane, and scattered across the star dust park: hundreds of body bags beneath angelic-white Dogwood branches that wave like sick hands.

It is Spring *and the winds are calling*.

The children have brought their supplies: some bundles of string, and rusty cafeteria knives. These children haven't forgotten how to have fun. After all, what would children be if they did not know how to play?

They move closer, surrounding the bodies in their black bags. They begin carving black diamonds out of the bags, and then they poke small holes around the ends of the holes, securing them with their string. And as the winds whip about them; the children laugh and laugh and laugh—

Oh, how they love flying kites at dusk!

The (Un)expected Second

Soon we will all be witness to

> The Time (so near to us)
> when Man & Woman will
> become so utterly confused
> that we will not be able
> to hear or see anything

& at this Pinnacle-Moment

> when we will be least likely
> to expect any sort of solution

Autumn's arrival will arrange

> the sharpest of tree branches
> to wrap-around & tear-thru the
> (plentiful) arteries of the
> (return) 'King of Kings'

& then all the avenues & alley-

> ways of The World will open
> wide like aroused mouths
> & through them will flow
> Great rivers of bile & shit

The Cracks We Slip Through

While picnicking in the park, a man spends all his time watching strangers passing by his spot. With already a firm understanding for his obsessive tendency to search for finite answers in infinite questions, the man begins staring deep into the strangers wandering eyes. He immediately senses from them some sort of unanimous joy.

The man silently asks himself, *how could this happiness make any sense when… after all… don't I worry constantly?* He then muses over this, and over his recent observations of the strangers. He then asks himself, *is not the Pleasure that these people extract from spending their free time, surrounded by all this nature, not even slightly deadened by Fear…The Great Fear…and inward suspicion that… they might have left their hallway doors open…before leaving their homes?*

The man tries hard to shake his manic thoughts. He returns to staring at the strangers. But, as new ones pass him, they seem more content than the ones before, and these fresh observations *of the same* spark within the man's mind, a very difficult question, and that is: *am I the only intelligent human being who has This Swallowing Fear of having left hallway doors open?*

And, when no one and nothing can answer his questions of silent introspection, the man becomes more frightened than ever in his whole life—frightened to the furthest depths of his core—though he does not know why.

The Goldfish

The Father crumbles fish flakes between his fingers. They drop: red, green, and yellow, in a dawdling dream-motion.

The Goldfish waits beneath the falling bits, like The Boy did, reaching to touch the confetti that fell from the blue skies of downtown Fourth of July parades.

The phone rings.

The Father picks up a newspaper.

The Mother runs into the other room to take the call.

The Boy stands and moves closer, leaning his forehead against the bowl.

He goes eye-to-eye with the fish. Its eyeballs swirl the color of spilt milk. Half of its right fin hangs from its side.

The Goldfish swims into the glass wall over and over again.

The Losing-Green Knowledge

In the hours before their pillows fell to the floor, before the showerhead dropped water in rhythmic thumps, as he sang songs that they had heard while preparing dinner the night before, before the toothpaste ooze stuck to the bathroom sink; she would lay motionless on the far side of the bed, with the sheets stripped down to her waist, staring at the yellow plastic stars scattered across the ceiling of their bedroom–the ones that had once held a strong nighttime glow–and she would study them with lost-green graveyard eyes (the color of laminated seaweed), and he would hear her breathing, like a land-found fish, and gasping The Unfamiliar, while she circled the outline protrusions of her breasts with unraveling fists,

she would roll over to him slowly, and he would stroke her damp cheeks, while she buried her eyes behind his hands, and she would cry, reporting to him the fragments from her Interstellar Dreams; about, how in those dreams, she had reached out for him, and she would tell him how The Galaxy's Council had handed him The Giant Calculator, and how he froze over the screen; unable to calculate The Distance Between their fingertips, and she would say *I lost you…I lost you…I lost you again…I…* and it was as if she thought he could comprehend her New & Uncharted World of Trees That Bled The Sounds Of Mercury, where colors were experts In Chemistry, and finally she would roll over, swallowing her tears, and say *I lost you for good* before closing her eyes, and going to sleep, to do it all over again in the morning.

No Less of a Citizen

Climbing up the train car ladder, the man asks himself, *why in god's name do I do what I do?* At the thought of the most rational answers to this question, the man quickly recoils from all thinking. He tries to shake all thoughts and questions from his mind, at least for a moment longer, until he can cross over the threshold, and step into the train car.

Once inside, the man is immediately greeted by an attractive young woman dressed in a red uniform, and wearing a red felt cap on her head. She welcomes him with a smile, and with a high-shrilled voice she says, "Good Day!" The man can thinks that, *while her smile is pleasant enough, this smile is not truly intended for me, but is inspired by something more mysterious; by something deeply rooted in her memory.* The young woman's blatant superficiality angers the man greatly. He scoffs, shakes his head at her, and continues to walk down the aisle. As he walks, the man begins to think more on his position in life, and his heavy responsibilities. Under his breath, the man hisses, *but who could possibly forgive me for the things I do, even if I have to do them…tell me, who?*

The train car has come alive; breathing excitement. To the passengers, what's to come is all new, shiny, and unexpected. Many of them are traveling out of the state for the first time in their pathetic lives; he included among this group, but different. The train car is filled to the brim with an inexperienced expectation of something; something invisible that they believe will soon be better than yesterday's life.

The man becomes extremely agitated with all of this uncontrolled schoolyard energy, and he reaches into his trench coat pocket for the ticket. When he retrieves it, he stands still, and studies the black numbers. He quickly translates his seat assignment. He then glances from side to side, before mentally connecting his seat number with the cabin ahead of him. Once he reaches his cabin, the man pauses outside the door, as he always does in this situation, and takes in a deep breath. The man knows that he must be prepared, no matter how every situation might present itself. The man exhales, and then opens the door. When the man sees what he sees, he gasps loudly.

Inside the cabin sits his youngest daughter and her toddler boy. The man's grandson looks up and waves to him. The man shouts and falls backwards against the door. He starts to cry, and he thinks *could they possibly begin to understand why I have to do what I will have to do? No! No! No, this can't be happening…but, this is what is asked of me, and what must be done!*

The man– weary with sadness, desperation, and an aching sense of loyalty– closes his swollen eyes, and quickly unties the sash of his trench coat, until the whole thing drops to the floor. It is then that they see his body, covered from head to toe with hundreds of bananas. And the daughter understands what will come next... and it is then that the real screaming begins...

The Small Town Musical

The old woman thought things had improved. She thought that she was getting better by now. She thought it all had stopped for good. She thought that she would finally have some peace at last. But, when the polka music inside her head started playing again, she began to scream like she was burning alive.

"E-N-O-U-G-H," she told herself, and she shook her head like a seizure. And, with that one decisive thought, she jumped up from her green, raggedy sofa. The old woman fled her double-wide in a storm, blowing by all the young bleach-blondes, who were tanning their tight, near-naked, hairless bodies beneath the strong summer sun.

The old woman ran down the middle of the trailer park's gravel avenue; until the gravel gave way to HWY 18, just outside of her park. She turned left, and followed the highway for a flat half mile, to the small town's general store. Yet, because the woman was so old and frail, she could not run the entire way; sometimes she would walk, and many times she would stop to catch her breath.

All the while, the old woman told herself that there was no music playing in her head. "Nothing...," she whispered. But, the polka music grew louder and louder. No matter how hard she tried to convince herself, it was impossible to deny.

Once inside the general store, the old woman walked straight for the man behind the counter, shaking her head violently. She never smiled at the man, and she never greeted him; but, she asked for a hammer and one long nail. The man behind the counter, who loathed being called 'cashier,' was glad she did not address him in that way, and exchanged his goods for her money. And, as he did this, he too did not smile nor say a 'good day' to the old woman.

When their exchange was complete, the old woman turned from the man behind the counter. She left the general store, without looking back, and followed HWY 18, for a flat half mile home. As she walked, she sang Christmas carols, to pass the time, and to get her mind off the polka music. But, her caroling could not drown out the music in her head.

When the old woman had reached the yard, she looked around to see if anyone was watching her, holding the hammer and nail. She was comforted by the solitude of the park, but there was no silence. From within her head, the polka music was blaring so loudly, and with so much intensity, that she began to sob uncontrollably.

The old woman stood still, outside her front steps, and thought, "No, no more of This Hell; not anymore!" She entered her trailer, alone, and slammed the aluminum door behind her.

THERE   WAS   NO   ECHO.

WHEN   YOU   ARE   DEAD
You   hear no   echoes
WHEN YOU ARE DEAD
You   hear no   echoes
WHEN YOU ARE DEAD
You   hear no   echoes
WHEN YOU ARE DEAD
You   hear no   echoes
WHEN YOU ARE DEAD
You   hear no   echoes
WHEN YOU ARE DEAD
You   hear no   echoes
WHEN YOU ARE DEAD
You   hear no   echoes
WHEN YOU ARE DEAD
You   hear no   echoes
WHEN YOU ARE DEAD
You   hear no   echoes
WHEN YOU ARE DEAD
You   hear no   echoes
WHEN YOU ARE DEAD
You   hear no   echoes
WHEN YOU ARE DEAD
You   hear no   echoes
WHEN YOU ARE DEAD
You   hear no   echoes
WHEN YOU ARE DEAD
You   hear no   echoes
WHEN YOU ARE DEAD
You   hear no   echoes
WHEN YOU ARE DEAD
You   hear no   echoes
WHEN YOU ARE DEAD
You   hear no   echoes
WHEN YOU ARE DEAD
You   hear no   echoes
WHEN YOU ARE DEAD
You   hear no   echoes
WHEN YOU ARE DEAD
You   hear no   echoes
WHEN YOU ARE DEAD

You   hear no   echoes

To Say Just a Few More Things about the Desert [1]

1, 3, 5, 7, 9, 2, 4, 6, 8...The Desert Exists Within An Infinite Blur of Sound and Color – *so much sound and color blurring all at once* – there is nothing more than an all encompassing gray-grain silence. Everything, at first, appeared to be fuzzy and lacking definite shape.

To Say Just a Few More Things about the Desert [10]

10, 12, 14, 16, 18, 11, 13, 15, 17…*do I lack a definite shape, like these cacti?*

I remember that I have a travel size mirror in my backpack. I retrieve the mirror, and hold it up in front of me. I see. My face is plastic. There are deep fissures where my forehead is starting to crack under the intensity of The Desert Sun that rapes me, relentlessly.

Atop my head sits a paper, cone-shaped, birthday hat with fat silver stars. The hat is attached by a string, wrapped around my jaw. The paper hat is crooked in a tilt; positioned on the far right side of my head.

I see *something* else . . .

To Say Just a Few More Things about the Desert [19]

19, 21, 23, 25, 27, 20, 22, 24, 26...From deep within the fissures of my forehead, I can see tiny_____, poking out into the sunlight. They are...*FINGERS?* ...popping out of my face, trying to escape from me! Yes, yes, there are stubborn, stubby little fingers that are attempting to push a way through the large cracked gaps, desperately trying to peel back the plastic layers of my face...in order to....in order to, escape?

...I can hear THEM chanting recess songs from deep within me; The Children... and, from beneath the chorus line, I hear screams. Their voices are ungodly. Their voices are otherworldly!

What pain they must feel!

There are **children** trapped   inside my face   !
There are children **trapped**   inside my face   !
There are **children** trapped   **inside my face**   !!!
There are children **trapped**   inside my face   !
There are **children** trapped   inside my face   !
There are children **trapped**   **inside my face**   !!!
There are **children** trapped   inside my face   !
There are children **trapped**   inside my face   !
There are **children** trapped   **inside my face**   !!!
There are children **trapped**   inside my face   !
There are **children** trapped   inside my face   !
There are children **trapped**   **inside my face**   !!!
There are **children** trapped   inside my face   !
There are children **trapped**   inside my face   !
There are **children** trapped   **inside my face**   !!!
There are children **trapped**   inside my face   !
There are **children** trapped   inside my face   !
There are children **trapped**   **inside my face**   !!!
There are **children** trapped   inside my face   !
There are children **trapped**   inside my face   !
There are **children** trapped   **inside my face**   !!!
There are children **trapped**   inside my face   !
There are **children** trapped   inside my face   !
There are children **trapped**   **inside my face**   !!!
There are **children** trapped   inside my face   !
There are children **trapped**   inside my face   !
There are **children** trapped   **inside my face**   !!!
There are children **trapped**   inside my face   !
There are **children** trapped   inside my face   !
There are children **trapped**   **inside my face**   !!!

When the grey mist broke,
You took-off, running for the sea

I remember being jarred awake
By the thunderous squawking of birds
That sounded like the musical fragmentation
For a stirring symphony on mass-mutilation

I titled my swollen eyes up curiously
Toward the spreading orange-rusted sky
Squinting from time to time to deflect
The factories' frozen ashes that fell down
Across my raw cheeks like drifting sleet

Under January's deformation spell
Beneath a suffocated winter moon
I watched thousands of black-out
Silhouettes circling me overhead
Before nose-diving one-by-one
Into the giant mouths of smokestacks

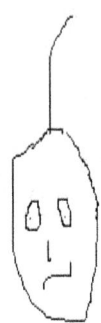

[Invocation to
THE MUSE]

Solitary Volcano
Solitary Volcano
Solitary Volcano
Solitary Volcano
Solitary Volcano
Solitary Volcano
Solitary Volcano

I call to you, but
No-
One
Answers

Me

No   *One*
(w*a*nts to)
Re-
Member

THE VORTEX
&MEMORY

I've spent
a q u a r t e r of
my life,   living
underneath   the
bathtub,   reading
E   Z   R   A

PO   U   N   D

pRIMA
R-i-l-y
E.P   's
                    V - O
                    R - T
                    E - X
                    THEORY

Hey,   ____   No[w]
You   all   s[h]o[u] l d
See   the[m] all
You   [k]now them
They   s[h]oul[d]   you
              see   ___
___
[K]Now   yoU,   He[y]!

In times such as these
nobody wants
to be associated
with Ezra Pound.

So, of course,

These NObodies
        these rats of comfort
        these plagiarists of Formalism
        these 'New Formalist' Professors,
                professing
                their Program of Literary Politics
& All these robotic scholars, feeding on
                Spoon-fed accessibility
(a n t h o l o g i e s)
These goddamn nobodies want

N   O   T   H   I   N   G

To do with me; The Boy
Who reads & chants POUND'S lines
Like they were _____&____&____&____, etc.!
NORTON SAYS NORTON
SAYS NORTON SAYS
NORT ONSAY SNORTON
SAYS NOR TO NSAYS
NOR TONSAYS NORTON
SAYS NOR TO NSAYS
NORTON SA YSN ORTON
SAYSNO RTONS AYS
NORTON SAYSNO RTON
SAYS NORTON SAYS

ANY -

      WAYS

|

      wAs

ANY -

      WAYS

/

      wAs

   A
   -
L   O
N   E
   -

     For
     ~~ALL THIS~~

        TI -
        M E

<u>W/ all of E.P.'s books</u>
        &

THEORIES, underneath
the bathtub, for what
I figured would be
a lifetime. And then,
there you were; then
you CAME. You,
TO my SURPRISE,,,,,,,,,,?,,,,,,,,,,,,,,,,,,,,,,,
,,,,,,,,,,,,,,,?,,,?,,
,,,?,,,,,,,,,,,,,,,,,,,,
,,,,,,,?,,?,,,,,,,

The
New
You
Who
Knew
            Nothing

                    of
            Pound's [Late] Politics,
            Imagist/Vortex/Objectivists Theories,
                & 'briliante' Epic poetry;

Therefore

I knew you
Could not
Judge me   NOT
                            Based
                            -ON

The Life & Work
& Passions of Ezra   Pound

/

-

Alas, Alas, Alas, Alas,

FIN-ALLY! It was
one night   ,

That night, you
On accident/ accidentally
Bumped into me;
An action that had been
Sparked and fueled by
The wall-clawing boredom
That resulted from applying
Expensive Conditioner to your
Abnormally long hair. And instead
Of facing the boredom, you
Decided it would be better
To take a swim around my (?)
/ your / tub,

In my bathtub, I read, &
in my bathtub, I breathe, but,
never in my bathtub do I__

_____

N   e   V   e   R

_____

& that is when
        The tips of
Your fingers touched
        Mine. "Fingertips," you
Would later say, "That
Sprouted out of the clogged
        Drain like lukewarm-
Green peanut shells birthed
        From Southern-
Home   soil…"

Eventually

You

Pulled

My Body

Free

From the drain,

But not without

A Great strain

....
Was Ezra
Pound's books,
Books that you
Knew nothing about,
That initially held me back
From exiting the bathtub.

                        &
                                You
                                Gently
                                Urged
                                Me to leave
                                The books behind
                        &   "come on out of it," & so
Trusting you,

                                I did just that.
                        &
Over the edge
of the bathtub   we both went,
You & I

On(to) the linoleum.

Loo   mis(s)
    ::   *where in my memory, is*
Loo   mis(s)
    ::   *where in my memory, is*
Loo   mis(s)
    ::   *where in my memory, is*
Loo   mis(s)

- - - **Soon** - - -

We were sitting
In a/my/your dusty living
Room in my/your dusty
Furniture, facing each other.
We stared curiously.
We stared in silence.
I was cold. You
See[me]d comfortable.

Somewhere
There was

70

Something
There was
De[finite]ly some-
Thing there
I had wanted
So terribly
To tell you – Some-
Thing – and I knew then
That it did not matter
That I had never known you
Before meeting in the bathtub.
Some
Thing,
Some-thing,   some
                               [more]   [than]   [that]

            this
    'THING'

Had *RUSHED into THE VORTEX*…
So-me-thing me-aning-ful, Or-

Igin-al, & or-nate; a de-InFinite rush of
                               Image,
                    Sound,
                               Life,
                          Economics,
                History,
                               Homer,
                    News
                          clippings,
            E M O T I O N S

no, YES, no… Certainly
Within the vortex, *YES,*
Something felt,
A-thing that
Was *Living and worthy to live*--

            this
    'THING.'

& stud-
Ying you,
Watching

A lone
Water drop
Let fall from the tips
Of your golden hair,
Snaking
Down the inward-
Curve of your neck,
& Slide down your chest,
Over your breast,
& Puddle in your lap; I knew.
I knew that *that* some-thing was
Very important, urgent – this
Something I had to tell
You...turned to be
A non-remembered thing: a
Lost cause, blank-
Blank, a shot of
      Water through the veins.

It didn't matter
      Not
                Any-
                      More
No matter
How hard
I searched
There was
Nothing
There

I scrambled all of my thoughts
For a way to say *just* what I could not

Absolutely nothing surfaced
Within me I sat, feeling bitter.
& that was when
You turned your face
Away from mine,
& You yawned
(without covering your mouth),
& You stared down the hall
-way, & I knew that this,
Whatever it may have been,
This bond?,
Had come all to
No-Thing.

EZRA   I WANTED TO
KILL MYSELF   EZRA I WANTED
TO SHOW ME HOW TO KILL MY

             [[[self]]]

But, more than all of that
                              I wanted to
Burn all books   I wanted to
Drain all
        The Atlantic
        Pacific &
        The Baltic
              too
                              I wanted to
Dive head-first
Into THE VORTEX
& be swallowed up.   I wanted to
Suddenly be
Impregnated with
The knowledge
of the Past, History?,
Hiz-Toe-Ree.   I wanted to
Speak the language
Of the future – sign
Nonsensical symbols
 –Nothing.   I wanted to

Rot into nothingness.

But more than wanting _____
I wanted most
To remember that
Some-THING
Important
That I had always
Wanted to share with you…
For you…because of you…
Something for the Word…

                    p   r   a   y

While You Sleep in the City

The barn echoes with death. The boy knows this all too well. He knows, because he sleeps out there, alone, in the barn.

The day before yesterday, upon waking, the boy saw that long ropes had been tied tightly around the wooden rafters overhead. From the knotted loop-ends of each rope, strangers' bodies hanged limp and heavy, like industrial-size sandbags. And when there came the occasional strong gust of wind plowing through the gutted barn, the corpses swung slow like giant brass pendulums, gently thumping against the dusty walls.

At first, the boy was terrified by what he saw before him. But, at the same time, he was strangely comforted by the surreal sound-beats that were being produced by the swaying of their bodies, and the low hissing of the taut ropes that held them by their gray- wrinkled necks. And as it were, these grotesque sounds brought the boy reassurance a sudden sense of serenity, like one gets from listening to the internal workings of a failing grandfather clock, as it whispers, as it clicks: Tic…**Toc**…Tic…**Toc**…Tic…**Toc**!

THE SIDE EFFECTS OF REVIEWING 'NEW FORMALISM' POETRY

One evening, after having spent two weeks on my red sofa, devouring thousands of lines of bitter iambic pentameter, I stood up and glanced around.

I knew what I had to do.

I felt it coming over me, without a single syllable of self-restraint...

Like a savage tropical gust, I began overturning all the furniture in my small apartment: the half-shredded red sofa; the mold-spotted leather recliner; the ash covered coffee table; the thin metal bookshelves, filled with 99¢ paperbacks; the barren kitchen table; the slowly-imploding platform bed; the cracked chest of drawers; the orange coat rack; my stuffed & plastered cat, Veruca Salt.

Five more minutes and I was out of breath and in a pant, when four thoughts rose to the surface, to occupy my wild mind:

1) Did Lope de Vega ever love the 16 yr old Isabel de Urbina?

2) The benefits of not owning cable.

3) How the mortal male architects of organized religion *might* have birthed the idea– the silly illusion– of 'virginity' and 'chastity' for the unwed, in hopes of keeping women underfoot…and how other mortal male myths relate to Today's society.

4) The chemical nature of the AA alkaline battery.

Craving *only* finite answers, I sat in the middle of the bedroom floor and lit a cigarette. I picked up a framed portrait of marbles (hidden under the bed for emergencies), and started to masturbate to the electric array of brilliant colors.

Before The Spinning Color Wheel Becomes Our Primary Source of Energy

From the wastebasket in the far left corner of the living room, a To Do Note from Friday, August 30th–a piece of notebook paper that had been crumple-crushed and molded by my mind into a stone–is now soaking up all of the television's slow-spilling energy. That which was once stone is now taking the form of a giant clam shell, and I spot something else that cannot be ignored.

Inside the mouth of the giant clam shell is a slightly less large purple pearl... and I am confused, because this pearl is no ordinary pearl. This pearl is radiating The Static of Sunday, and buzzing The Neon of Tuesday. And it is not much longer before I accept my new fate. I must burn The Calendar of Regrets!

losingMACRO

T   co   em,   b   sh. W
    le.   a   n. O   st   e
    er, p
thi   an   b   or   nd   ag.
    k w   r,
O   ev   ght.   ti :   L
    3,8,or 9.

Youth Questioning the Sun

Having no father to advise him, and devastated by the recent village fires that had killed his family by destroying their home, the boy raised his blackened face and arms toward The Sun, and asked, "Well, what comes next for me and, *this*, my miserable life?" The Sun (not being particularly fond of questions, and the boy's unfaithful curiosity) set his holey clothes aflame.

THE LAST THREE DAYS OF YOUR FINAL STARVATION

The first feeling is still unknown. The second feels like denim being torn between your teeth. The third is like falling down a Giant's mouth—WIDE-OPEN-ABYSS—until you are suspended in mid-air, as if tied to the end of a rope, in the middle of his throat.

.

Triple-Checking My Long Division Revisions

It was as if I was safe for a   time
Predictable even
Through simple routines

Or at least I thought

All my thoughts were   sparked
By the Rock that gassed
Beaten-blue-eye   smoke
Twisting forth from a hole
Shaped like a watermelon   seed
         that fed
The deformed nostril(s) of   my soul

& the smoke spiraled off
as infinite as the sea   maybe

All I sought was   swallowed
         by shadows

<<much, much later>>

To be exposed by the color wheel   that spun-off
Mechanical sounds associated with   my doubts

Like watching the giant metal teeth
Of a rusted escalator   rising
To pull you away

         falling

         failing

         (flailing)

         fail

Mr. X in House Slippers

I.

During one of his many manic fits, the old man [Mr. X] had gone and planted 147 cabbages in his cramped backyard, because he had recently lost all sexual desire for his wife [Mrs. X] who cannot even begin to comprehend her husband's many eccentric fascinations [fetishes].

II.

Whether or not you knew his age/hometown/eye color/food allergies, and whether or not you knew of his great admiration for the illustrators of children's books, and whether or not you knew of *his* algebraic formula—he *does* have one, copyrighted, that is customized to equal his middle name—in the end, it doesn't matter much to him...

What is most significant, to him, is that you are acutely aware of the diverse [oh-so-extravagant!] personalities constantly emitted from his nose, arms, and toes.

III.

Alone in his garage, usually around Midnight, when Mr. X laughs, it sounds like green Guam sand [Raytheon Co. microwave oven (1946) --- white oak acorns --- George Foreman Grills © --- newborn babies] burning.

Some Same Redundant Loopholes

EXPLORE THE ZOO for your Doctoral Focus in _____Translation, and watch what you get in return! **OR,** better yet… strip a wild fox of all its cunningness, then **DISASSEMBLE** an origami paper crane, and (*finally*) pluck your three initials from the eyebrows of **A DONKEY**.....................................*Some-of-THAT* is what you are left with

FAMILY MATTERS

Your girlfriend flips the kitchen light switch. Her hand reaches into the cabinet, where you sit, for a late night snack. She touches you; suit-cased inside. You are sawing your wrists with a rusty box cutter. Without questioning if this might be a cry for help or an act of boredom, she drives you across three states to the home you grew up in.

THERE, *a pig in flight*, spinning out of the trapdoor beside the linen closet. You duck and look. The hallways are greyer than you remembered them being. Shadows swell the triangles behind doors left ajar.

Your mother is behind you, blue-skinned and on her knees, crying. Her eyes are the color of swirling spilt milk. Tiny tadpoles swim through the gaps where her pupils used to be. She points to the pig and begs you to report him for sipping the last of her green tea.

Glass shatters. You spit

and turn. The pig is crawling up the walls, mechanically, squealing in clumsy pursuit of the rotting-apple chandelier hanging from the ceiling where flies collaborate with one another. They hoard what they feel is rightfully theirs.

Your mother laughs loudly. The flies swarm in black clouds around the pig's eyes. He falls from the chandelier and through the mahogany floorboards below. Dust plumes all around you and your mother is doing back-flips down the dark hallway.

Your best friend is dancing alone in the guest room, waving a handgun above his head.

ALL THRIVE

The Great Mentor, frailed premature, backleaned against the sidewinds strong, holding upside down an inkpen, so The Boy could study the draining ink downslide through the glass shaft– *fragile! fragile! fragile*–and tipout as purple blue waves in the wind: a lullaby nightmare occurring; re-occurring; recurring.

Almost Thriving

Balloon goes pop! **LET::PASS::OPEN::GO**. In The Winter, you can see the telephone's gasps, forming in the air. *Test it out, why don't you? There!* Compact disk: Mozart: on repeat. Compact disk: Mozart: writhing in the dust. The last worm in the last of books tells me to witness. The apple has been sliced and diced. The Great Mentor said of Life, Fiction, "The way in which you **ENTER** [fill in the blank], is the way in which you will **EXIT** [fill in the blank with whatever you've 'entered' in the line above]."

What I Saw When I Thought I Was Having a Heart-Attack

Dead-ends and other street signs led me towards The Last Exit Highway Horizon turning pink pussy into brown meat with a crackle and pop on the stovetop hot flashes of The Woman expecting blue-skinned babies to wash up silently with the stain-red tide across a country road layered with black-ice frosting.

The Disappearing Act

This boy wasn't a lawyer, besides; he was far too young and uneducated to be fit for any proper profession. This boy liked to rub his hands over his crotch, especially after running through the woods. This boy was told that he looked like a diseased raccoon, but talked like a lawyer. This boy would smell his crotch-sweaty hand and imagine far away towns full of familiar people.

This boy was not a very big boy. This boy was a great lover of animals, especially dogs. This boy thought he just might be the tiniest boy in the world. This boy loved dogs so much, that when no one was around to interrupt him, he would kiss them passionately, using his tongue. This boy couldn't ever stop the bigger boys from pulling his shorts down around his ankles.

This boy's mother once threw a pot of boiling water at his head when she caught him down in the basement, loving on the hunting dogs. This boy said nothing when the bigger boys shoved a branch inside of him. This boy was sometimes an angry boy, especially at weekend yard sales. This boy was found in the woods by his father with the end of a branch planted deep inside of his ass.

This boy, when no one was watching, would urinate and defecate on the things that were for sale: glass ashtrays, silverware, empty bookshelves, second-hand sofas, and manual typewriters. This boy's father laughed at him, when he found him in the woods, and called him a Patsy.

This boy made sure his mother and father were deep asleep before he took off all of his clothes, walked out the back screen-door, and followed the moonlight to the middle of the lake…

....and, all that follows that, follows this....

Three weeks have passed, and the old man hasn't left his bed; not for anything.

Leaving my bed, he thinks, *is an impossibility...it just won't happen*! But, 'it'–his leaving or not leaving bed–is all a matter of choice for the old man, and this he cannot comprehend. He has stopped working, stopped walking, stopped talking, stopped eating, stopped drinking, and stopped reacting.

Outside of occasionally thinking, the old man has stopped existing. He questions this every day, and he thinks, *I am still very much alive, if only by a thread...See, I have a batch of children, and I breathe, do I not?*

But what of the children, his children, what might they think of their incapacitated father? From the kitchen their screams travel like lightning down the hallway, echoing through the master bedroom, where the old man has buried himself beneath skeletal sheets.

He thinks,
I can't!
        He thinks,
        I just can't!
He thinks,
I can't!
        He thinks,
        I just can't!
He thinks,
I can't!

Yesterday, the children fought over a pair of pink roller skates. Last week, the children debated over the dismal states of medical insurance and national economics, and their debate was ended with a knifing to the side of the oldest, done by the youngest. Today, the children wrestle over a piece of stale bread.

None of the children think nor mention anything of the old man.

FLIGHT

Last night he had the most peculiar dream of his young life. He remembers getting out of bed, and leaving his house. He remembers walking through town, until he reached the giant water tower. He remembers climbing up the tower, and taking deep breaths while he looked over the town below him. He remembers leaping over the edge of the tower, and he remembers flying. He remembers all that he saw: his church, his elementary school, his family's cotton fields, and his parents' house.

While he was floating over the roof, he remembers hearing terrible cries coming from his bedroom. But, before he could begin to translate the screams as his or another, he was awake in his bed again. And, once fully awake, he remembers being able to see with the greatest of clarity, even in the darkest hours of the morning. In the corner of his bedroom, he remembers what his father looked like, curled into a shaking ball, beneath the window, clawing out his eyes.

To Wherever They Might Go By Day

Whenever all this ends
Don't cry for what is not. . .
But   promise me that you will
Set my wooden frame aflame

Then   just sit and be still
And listen for their applause
The thumping of a thousand moths wings
Together and at once

In the night
If you wait
They will find our glow

Watch them descend one-by-one
Fluttering out from the dried veins
Of Spanish moss that hangs from
The toothpick branches of splintering trees

The moths will dance between
The purple flames that lick the sky

Above me
Dropping
Eventually

To lift my body up from the ash
To take me away

"Where Have I Been?"

Fireworks crack, pop-pop, and fizzle over this beach town, then, no more.

The screen door groans as I enter my son's apartment. I turn on the fan to cut the stench of whiskey and stale piss. Orange plastic pill bottles lead me to his bedroom. I open the door, letting in light from the hallway. The light casts shadows between his ribs. He is belly up on the floral print mattress choking on vomit. I sit on the mattress, resting his head on my lap. I run my hands over his face, wiping his lips.

He has been dying for a long time.

THE HARD TRUTHS ABOUT LIVING AND DYING

While you are living, the meaning of your life is formed from that which seems to be the most pleasant [or profitable] to your imagination-- you are still breathing. When you die there is no breath, and your life's true purpose is finally realized. There is absolutely no meaning, and there is a great disappointment that can never be eradicated.

About Zachary C. Bush

Zachary C. Bush, 25, is a writer of poetry and prose. He holds a BA in Creative Writing & Linguistics from Georgia Southern University. He is currently pursuing an MFA in Poetry and Short Fiction from the City College of New York. His first full-length collection of poetry, <u>At Swan Decapitation</u>, is to be published by *VOX Press* (Oxford, MS*).* <u>Angles of Disorder</u> is his second collection. Bush resides in Jersey City, New Jersey.

Made in the USA
Monee, IL
07 July 2026

56544775R00057